ENGAGE!

How to Attract and Inspire a High-Performance Team

BRENT HULTMAN

Engage! How to Attract and Inspire a High-Performance Team
Copyright © 2020 by Brent Hultman.

All rights reserved. No part of this publication may be reproduced, distributed, or transmitted in any form or by any means, including photocopying, recording, or other electronic or mechanical methods, without the prior written permission of the author, except in the case of brief quotations embodied in critical reviews and certain other noncommercial uses permitted by copyright law.

Jones Media Publishing
10645 N. Tatum Blvd. Ste. 200-166
Phoenix, AZ 85028
www.JonesMediaPublishing.com

Disclaimer:

The author strives to be as accurate and complete as possible in the creation of this book, notwithstanding the fact that the author does not warrant or represent at any time that the contents within are accurate due to the rapidly changing nature of the Internet.

While all attempts have been made to verify information provided in this publication, the Author and the Publisher assume no responsibility and are not liable for errors, omissions, or contrary interpretation of the subject matter herein. The Author and Publisher hereby disclaim any liability, loss or damage incurred as a result of the application and utilization, whether directly or indirectly, of any information, suggestion, advice, or procedure in this book. Any perceived slights of specific persons, peoples, or organizations are unintentional.

In practical advice books, like anything else in life, there are no guarantees of income made. Readers are cautioned to rely on their own judgment about their individual circumstances to act accordingly. Readers are responsible for their own actions, choices, and results. This book is not intended for use as a source of legal, business, accounting or financial advice. All readers are advised to seek the services of competent professionals in legal, business, accounting, and finance field.

Printed in the United States of America

ISBN: 978-1-948382-01-4 paperback
JMP2020.2

CONTENTS

Introduction 1

Chapter 1   The Difference between Conditioned and Innate Strengths..3

                We're All Conditioned 8
                Conditioning Can Be a Curse or a Treasure. 10
                Innate Strengths Aren't Work 13

Chapter 2   Your Personal Why 17

                My Journey from Chasing Other's Why to Pursuing My Why..17
                Why We Are Frustrated 19
                What the Chase Does to Us 21
                The Strength of Knowing Your Why.............23

Chapter 3   Defining Personal Values...............................27

                What I Do Makes Me Feel Bad, So Why Do I Do It? 27
                What Are Values? 33
                What Are Your Values? 34
                Do My Values Matter? 35

Chapter 4	Understanding Organizational Why, Strengths, and Values 37
	What Did They Expect? 37
	Punished for Working Really Hard 42
	Do You Want Out? 43
	That's Not Cool versus That's Amazing.......45
Chapter 5	Aligning Personal and Organizational Why, Strengths, and Values 47
	I Was in the Wrong Place 47
	Do You Have to Compromise Everything to Succeed?..49
	Why You're Exhausted 51
	It Just Got Easy! 52
Chapter 6	Understanding the Why, Strengths, and Values of Others on the Team..................................55
	Everything is a Team Sport! 55
	Disengaged—What's with the Attitude? 61
	The In-Crowd and the Rest 62
	There's Hope If We All Lean In....................63
Chapter 7	Your Personal Alignment..............................65
	Finally, It All Clicked 65
	Your Personal Why 66
	Your Personal Strengths..............................67
	Your Personal Values......................................69
	Align with Your Teammates and Organizational Why, Strengths, and Values..69

Chapter 8	Establishing and Maintaining Clear Communication and a Culture That Nurtures High-Performance 71
	But Can We Sustain This? 71
	So, You Think You're Communicating 75
	That Isn't What You Expected? 78
	How You'll Know That You're Effective 79

Chapter 9	Too Good to Be True 83
	The Few 83
	It's Simple, but It's Not Easy 84
	Tend to It or It'll Become a Weed Patch 86

References 89

About the Author 91

INTRODUCTION

When I started plans for writing this book in 2018, the economy was strong, and the biggest problem most US companies seemed to be facing was attracting and retaining people in order to keep up with the growth and demands of their businesses. As I finish this project, we're in the middle of the global COVID-19 crisis. At this moment, economic and social futures are uncertain, as world leaders and businesspeople around the world work to bring us out of this pandemic and to define "normal" once it's over.

I'm confident that doing the work this book invites you to do for yourself and for your organization will be as important as ever once we recover from this crisis. Considering the present and future socioeconomic climate, this information will be of great value to individuals, leaders, and teams.

The subconscious mind has only two goals: to keep you safe and to avoid pain. People often say that the two goals are to keep you safe and to make you happy. I suggest that safety and pain avoidance are more foundational. I mention this now because throughout this book I'll share my personal story of growth. Being safe and avoiding pain takes different forms for each of us. Most of us spend our time believing that we're in charge of our lives and that we're making logical choices. The emotions in our subconscious trigger behaviors that feel safe. Emotions may even feel like they won't only avoid pain but might make us happy. However, many people aren't happy.

We'll explore the challenges that we all face when we accept safety and pain avoidance without discovering a purpose for doing what we do. I'll challenge you to do the work to know your true self and then to join others in creating high-performance teams that take you and your teammates to levels of accomplishment and satisfaction that you might not have imagined possible.

CHAPTER 1

The Difference between Conditioned and Innate Strengths

I knew I was being an ass, but I didn't know it was okay to stop.

For years I felt that the old expression "Lead, follow, or get out of the way!" was a great motto for success. I felt that this was the key to success in pretty much every situation. I told myself it was my obligation to step up and to get things done. My behavior gave others the impression that if people didn't like how I was leading, that was too bad. I got things done. But, at times, I was an ass.

I didn't really like being that way. There were many times that arrogant, domineering behavior seemed to be the only way to get things done. I justified this behavior by telling myself that we all have options. If people didn't like how I wanted something done, they could get out of the way. It never occurred to me that I had the option of not behaving like an ass. There were a lot of situations where I didn't see room for anyone else to lead—after all, I was already doing that. As a leader, I needed followers. People who didn't follow were in my way, so they needed to get out of the way.

When I was in the Army, the system allowed me to hold my belief that "Lead, follow, or get out of the way!" was a great motto. I was smart enough to follow those above me in the chain of command (follow). I expected the people who reported to me to follow because they were below me in the chain of command (lead). There were even occasions where "get out of the way" was a pretty clear option, because people who didn't follow could end up court martialed. I was young and figuring out how to lead and how to get things done by trial and error. Most of the time it seemed that what I was doing worked and pleased those who were leading me.

I had grown up being told, "Children are to be seen and not heard." Adults told me what to do (they led, I followed). Failure to stick to this plan resulted in punishment. I would try to keep quiet and be a good little follower, even when I wanted to speak up and lead. My desire to lead was strong as far back as I can remember. My elementary school years were tough. I saw that my teachers left a lot of room for a smart little leader to step up. I now see that they saw a little smart-ass, not a smart little leader.

My first memory of a face-to-face leadership conflict was when I was in first grade. It was late December. The teacher was asking the kids what they hoped Santa would bring them for Christmas. (This was in the days that we had the Pledge of Allegiance every morning and talked about Christmas in the classroom.) When I was in kindergarten, my mom had shared that Santa wasn't real and that she and my dad bought my Santa gifts. Since I had some information that I felt would enlighten my fellow first graders, I announced to the class, "Santa's not real. It's your mom and dad."

Faster than I could say "Ho ho ho!" my teacher grabbed me by the arm and pulled me out into the hall. She shook her finger in my face and said, "You know that there's no Santa Claus, and I know that there's no Santa Claus, but they"—pointing to the classroom door—"don't know that there's no Santa Claus! Never say anything like that again!"

As I look back, I now realize that this, and many other experiences from my formative years, shaped me for better and for worse; my personality formed and conditioned behaviors helped to develop my ability to make my way through life. It's also clear that I wasn't very good at that being-seen-and-not-heard thing. This was one of many incidents where I wanted to take charge and ran afoul of the plans of adults, who wanted to remain in charge.

I embraced the idea that once I was an adult, it was my turn to lead. By the way, back then I thought *lead* just meant being in charge and having others follow along with whatever I wanted to get done. I carried my childhood experiences to help shape my style of leadership in the Army. My thinking was, Soldiers are to be seen and not heard. In the Army at that time this approach worked well. (I suspect that there's a fair amount of this approach that's still practiced in the military. There's still a fair amount of this approach in business as well.)

I was promoted quickly and was responsible for people who were years older and much more experienced than I. This included men who had done a tour or two during the Vietnam war. I used what I knew, beginning with the assumption that I would lead and that they would follow. If that approach didn't work, I would work on the appropriate plan to get them out of the way. A lot of folks in the Army were much bigger asses than I was, so I didn't see a problem with this approach.

I've known a lot of people trapped feeling that there's one way to get things done and that being an ass may be the only option. Once I moved into the private sector, and people weren't in jeopardy of being court martialed for voicing that I was being an ass, I encountered direct negative feedback more often—I didn't like that. The worldview that my childhood and Army experiences shaped didn't always work.

I didn't like being seen as an ass, and I really didn't like being told that was how I was acting. My problem was still my perception that there were times that I had no choice. If

The Difference between Conditioned and Innate Strengths

there were times that I knew I was being an ass, how often was I being that way without realizing it?

As I look back, I'm sure that there were many occasions where I wasn't aware that this was how I came across. People either followed or got out of the way. I wasn't aware of the impression that I made, unless it was bad enough that someone would call me on my behavior. Most people try to avoid conflict. I suspect that there were times that people who wanted to avoid conflict also avoided me.

As I became more aware that being an ass may actually stand in the way of getting things done, I started to look for other options. When we feel that there's only one way to do something, it's often because we have been conditioned to feel this way. When conditioning is that strong and limiting, it's an indication that innate behavioral strengths have been shut down. Most people have an innate sense of how they're coming across to others. I was ignoring that to focus on getting things done. I believe most people who come across in negative ways are trapped in the belief that they have no choice. If that's you, keep reading—there is hope.

We're All Conditioned

If you took the same science classes that I did, the term *conditioning* may bring Pavlov's dogs to mind. Ivan Pavlov was a Russian physiologist. In the late 1800s, he worked with dogs to demonstrate that an external stimulus, such as a ringing bell, could cause a response that the stimulus would not originally have caused. Pavlov conditioned dogs to salivate when they heard a bell. A dog's innate response is to salivate when given meat, but through conditioning, they would salivate when they heard the bell, without being presented meat.

The way that Pavlov conditioned the dogs was to present them with meat and to make a sound at the same time. Once the dogs were conditioned to associate the sound with the meat, they would salivate without the meat when they heard the sound. The dogs were conditioned—that is, they learned to associate a sound with meat. Pavlov didn't invent conditioning; however, he was able to demonstrate how it works. Conditioning is part of the human experience as well. Pavlov demonstrated how conditioning takes place using dogs, but pretty much any organism can be conditioned.

We all have highly developed conditioned behaviors. Early childhood is full of conditioning. Without it you couldn't be an effective adult. You were conditioned to use the toilet along with countless other valuable things very early in life. Conditioning continues throughout life and

The Difference between Conditioned and Innate Strengths

makes it possible for you to perform new tasks and to adjust to changing situations. As you can see, conditioning isn't bad. It's when your conditioned behaviors dominate you, or block out an innate behavior that may be more appropriate to a particular situation, that you can get into trouble. Both your innate and conditioned behaviors can be strengths when they are used appropriately. Understanding all your behaviors and when to use your innate and your conditioned behaviors is what makes your behaviors into strengths. Any behavior can be a strength or a liability depending on when you demonstrate it.

Think of your behaviors as tools. You might compare any one of your behaviors to a twenty-pound sledgehammer. If you're aware that a behavior is, metaphorically, a twenty-pound sledgehammer, you understand when to engage that behavior. You'll only pick up that tool when you need it. If you need to demolish a wall, you'll grab that hammer and knock down the wall. As soon as you're finished with that task, you'll put the hammer down. If you're not aware of the influence of conditioning on your behavior, you may feel that you're a sledgehammer—that is, you may behave in an inappropriate manner because you're conditioned to certain behaviors that may not be the best choice for a particular situation. When it's time to knock down a wall, your sledgehammer behavior is appropriate, but if your next task is to give someone a pat on the back, they don't want you coming at them with a sledgehammer! As a result of your conditioning, you may have shut down behaviors that you could be using, limiting yourself to fewer options. Being unaware of your conditioned and innate behaviors limits you and is exhausting (imagine having to carry a twenty-pound sledgehammer around all the time). Knowing when to use conditioned behaviors and when to use innate behaviors turns both into strengths.

Conditioning Can Be a Curse or a Treasure

Learning conditioned behaviors so that they feel natural is a critical part in becoming an effective adult. Conditioning continues to be incredibly important throughout life as we encounter changing situations and need to master new skills. Your innate behaviors are also a vital part of who you are.

Your conditioning is a treasure. If you can identify your innate behavior-strengths, then you're in touch with your true self. When you can leverage both innate and conditioned behaviors as strengths, you're able to sustain high-performance.

A lot of your conditioning is stuff that you never need to think about. It becomes automatic. Conditioning is vital to all of us because it makes so much that you need to do possible. Imagine if you had to check an instruction book every time you needed to do anything that wasn't part of your innate wiring. That would make it impossible for you to function. However, when your conditioning suppresses your innate behavior-strengths, you're limiting yourself. When that happens, you limit your options. When I was being an ass to get things done, it was because I had accepted too few behavioral options.

Being limited in this way also drains your energy. It reduces your effectiveness and leads to stress and burnout. Rather than playing from who you naturally are (your innate strengths) and using your conditioning to get stuff done, you may end up trapped into feeling that there's only one way to get stuff done (even if you're being an ass or a sledgehammer!).

Understanding your unique conditioning and your innate strengths starts with an awareness of, what you might call, your free-range self. Your free-range self is the part of you that would exist without your conditioned behaviors. This is the stuff that you brought to the table starting from birth.

Imagine that you could divide your strengths into two toolboxes: one would contain your conditioning and the other your innate strengths. Once you have sorted them into the two toolboxes, you can see all your innate tools and all your conditioned tools.

If your free-range self was compliant and easy to deal with from infancy, then your conditioning may be more subtle. If you've always been told things such as "you were always an easy baby," your conditioning may have been a lot of positive reinforcement and rewards conditioned you to continue to be "easy." It's likely that you learned (were conditioned) to please parents and other adult authorities. If this was your childhood experience, it's probably your style as an adult. Being a people-pleaser as an adult may come at the expense of being your true self. If this is your story, it may be harder for you to sort your tools since your conditioning was more subtle. The positive reinforcement may have made it easy for you to feel that your conditioning is who you are. Conditioning that exaggerates innate behaviors can be a challenge because it's building on a part of your innate strengths. Your challenge, in this case, is that other parts of your innate behavioral potential may be stifled by this exaggerated set of behaviors.

On the other hand, if you were sent to the principal's office regularly and got into trouble starting at an early age, your conditioning may have been built more on punishment and negative consequences. That usually creates a clearer line between conditioning and innate behaviors. However, as an adult this conditioning may present as you being an ass. If you feel that you have to operate from your conditioned behaviors at the expense of ever engaging your innate behaviors—that is, if you don't feel that you're ever able to allow your true nature to determine your behavior—you will experience stress. If, deep down, you would rather do something that you feel someone else might judge you for doing, the tension between the behavior that you would like to demonstrate and one that you feel is the "right" choice creates stress. Sometimes this is a positive thing, because we all feel like doing selfish and inappropriate things from time to time. Gaining awareness of the appropriate use of both innate and conditioned behaviors is the key.

You turn both innate and conditioned behaviors into strengths once you're aware of both and choose when to use them as tools.

Innate Strengths Aren't Work

Your innate strengths aren't work. This is the stuff that just comes naturally. It feels like play rather than work and energizes rather than drains you. This can get complicated if you have a lot of conditioning and have lost sight of your innate strengths. It's easy to accept praise and reinforcement for your conditioning and then confuse that with innate strength.

Be careful. You may tell yourself that you're "a natural" at something because you've gotten reinforcement that has taught you to behave in a certain way. That's conditioning. Keep in mind that conditioning may be positive or negative: it modifies behavior either way.

Just to be clear, conditioning can reinforce innate behavior. Conditioning can also reinforce both positive and negative innate and conditioned behavior. Most behaviors are positive in the right time and place. Knowing how to lead without being an ass requires a balanced approach to using a wide range of behaviors.

Remember Pavlov's dogs? They didn't salivate when they heard a bell at first. Over time they associated the sound of the bell with meat. Ultimately, they were conditioned to respond to a sound in the same way that they responded to meat. Dogs don't have the mental capacity to understand choice in behavior beyond reward and punishment. Humans have a great deal of capacity to consciously choose between behavioral options.

It's not a bad thing to receive positive reinforcement, but remember that it reinforces your conditioning. Keep in mind that innate strengths don't feel like work. They energize you and empower you. You can use them to leverage your conditioning to accomplish more as you play from your innate strengths and intentionally engage your conditioning rather than salivating when someone else produces the right sound.

Think about that twenty-pound sledgehammer. If you know it's a tool (conditioning), you only pick it up when it's the appropriate tool for the task at hand. After you're finished knocking down a wall, you know that you can put the sledgehammer down and it will be there the next time that you need it.

The Difference between Conditioned and Innate Strengths

Once you're aware of both innate and conditioned strengths, you can play from your innate strengths and have more energy to use your conditioned strengths. When you know what you have in both of your toolboxes, you know that your innate strengths energize you and improve your conditioned performance as well. This balance makes both your conditioning and your innate strengths more effective because you're aware of your strengths and know how to intentionally leverage them to your greatest benefit. If you're like me, you've embarrassed yourself by demonstrating behavior that wasn't the best option. You probably felt that you just couldn't help yourself. When we lack clarity, unfavorable behavior happens a lot more often than it does when we're aware of our behaviors and when we use behaviors appropriately as tools to accomplish what we want to get done.

CHAPTER 2

Your Personal Why

My Journey from Chasing Other's Why to Pursuing My Why

In his bestselling book *Start with Why* (2009) Simon Sinek states: "WHY: Very few people or companies can clearly articulate WHY they do what they do." Sinek has written a lot about the importance of knowing why. Knowing why provides us with the energy to care about knowing how to do whatever we do.

As toddlers, "Why?" is a question that children frequently ask as they grow away from blind acceptance of what they're told. As children develop independent thought, they have a desire to understand why they should or shouldn't do whatever prompts the why question. Anyone who has kids or has worked with them knows that answering a kid's why question with "Because I said so!" isn't usually an effective response. Throughout this chapter, we'll explore why knowing your why is so important. As you may already see, you started searching for your why when you were a very young child.

It seems that wanting to know why is hardwired into us and becomes significant as we develop independent thought. Wanting to know why is an innate strength for all of us. We lose sight of this as conditioning begins to move us away from seeking our personal why toward being good followers. This starts as we learn to do what our parents expect and continues throughout our school years.

As toddlers we demonstrate great innate strength in seeking our own why apart from that of our parents and other adults. Our parents, on the other hand, often tire of seemingly endless streams of why questions. Especially when the why question is related to it being time for bed, parents may resort to the old "Because I said so!" out of frustration and fatigue. Whatever the reason, by the time I was an adult, like so many others I had stopped seeking to discover my own personal why.

As I was growing up, it seemed that it was often safer to look for why someone else wanted me to do whatever I was supposed to do. That didn't make me happy. This subconscious struggle is probably the cause of a lot of my trips to the principal's office and being disciplined at home. I wanted to be not only safe (do what I was told) but also happy (know why I should do something and decide for myself if I wanted to do it). This set up a conflict in my subconscious that led to frustration and stress. As I mentioned in the preceding chapter, when I was a kid my parents said, "Children are to be seen and not heard." Perhaps this led me to feel that the answer to "Why?" was found in seeking approval by doing what I was told. Maybe chasing another's why would both keep me safe and make me happy. At least chasing someone else's why might get me into less trouble. The problem was that it just didn't work for me to be that way. I ended up trading understanding my why for just getting things done.

Why We Are Frustrated

You may be seeing one of the problems frequently encountered when you don't know your personal why. When you're conditioned away from asking why and give up on defining your personal why, you're always operating from your conditioned strengths. Seeking your why is an innate strength, so it energizes you. Little kids never get tired of asking why. Often, we condition our kids to stop asking us why. You were probably conditioned away from that habit at an early age. Chances are your parents were raised with even less freedom to ask why than you were. The way people have been conditioned for generations would work very well if our innate need to know why weren't so strong.

As you grew up, your parents probably used both positive and negative conditioning to modify your behavior. You went to school and the curriculum probably emphasized how to do something without explain why you should do it. Schools tend to emphasize the what and the how side of things. This may have added to your existing conditioning that why questions weren't welcome.

In school, why you need to learn a given concept is that you must know how to do what you're told. You need to pass the test; you need to get good grades. If you bought into this and you learned to never ask why, you were probably told that you were a good kid. However, if your subconscious desire to know why got too close to the surface, you had probably earned a trip to see the principal. It's worth noting that your parents were being conditioned by the approval or scorn—positive or negative conditioning—that they felt from others as they figured out how to condition you to be a good kid and a successful adult.

Obviously, parents have to cut off endless why question games and schools need students to learn the how of things, often suppressing the why because of time or lack of necessity. This book isn't going to answer the age-old challenges of effective parenting or education. The point is, frustration about not knowing why starts early in life. By the time you're an adult, you may have stopped looking for a deep and satisfying answer to your personal why. Your frustration will continue to grow if you don't understand your purpose and the reason for your existence. Giving up on pursuing your why drains your energy and kills your imagination. This is why knowing your why is so important.

What the Chase Does to Us

Your conscious mind likes to think it's in control of everything. Thinking is what your conscious mind is all about. It thinks that you're a very rational and logical person. Whatever your conscious mind thinks, the reality is, as a human, you're actually driven by how things make you feel. Feeling is subconscious and unconscious mind stuff. Your conscious mind is good at realizing that a pesky feeling has caused a reaction to some stimulus. Your conscious mind provides a logical explanation for whatever you felt and did because of that feeling. So, your conscious mind thinks it's in control.

While your conscious mind is telling itself that it's in charge, your feelings continue to run wild. All those feelings have probably been conditioned so that you can get stuff done and fit in as a successful adult. You may feel like one of Pavlov's dogs if you think about this too much: don't. Just let your conscious mind tell you that feeling that way is irrational and that you're always in control of your thoughts (true) and feelings (yeah, right!).

Once you're conditioned to prioritize knowing how-to-do-what rather than knowing why, you may accept that knowing why doesn't matter. That might sound good, but there's a cost. You probably won't be able to avoid burnout if your actions lack the deeper purpose that comes from knowing your why. Getting good grades and earning money may satisfy your conscious mind, but they really don't provide a sustainable level of good feelings to counteract the frustration that continues to build in your subconscious over your unanswered personal why question.

Like me, you may attempt to chase an answer to why you're doing something by guessing why someone else wants it done. Employees often try to do whatever the boss wants. Business owners might assume that their why is to be good at getting other people to do stuff (see chapter 4 about your organizational why). Before you're ready for a business's why, you need to understand yourself and your why, strengths, and values. This is true if you're the newest intern, a CEO, or a business owner.

Trying to chase someone else's why usually just adds to your frustration. Your conscious mind wants to think there are a lot of reasons why things are happening. That's only logical. You can't think your way out of having an innate desire to know why you exist, why you're drawn to something, why you even want to get out of bed in the morning.

Even if you think you know someone else's why, none of those reasons answer the why question for you. This approach only fuels the subconscious conflict caused by not having your why question answered in the first place. Another problem with an unaddressed why is that since you may be looking for why in an environment where nobody knows why whatever is being done is important, how would you know if you found that illusive why? If none of the people around you understand their why, you and everybody else may be looking for a why that no one has identified. Remember, good grades and making money aren't the why for you or for your organization. They are a result of how-you-do-what.

The Strength of Knowing Your Why

To know your why is to know your purpose. When you're clear on your personal why, you know the reason for your existence. You get up and do things that feel like they matter. It's rewarding to know how-to-do-what because it gives you the skills to do stuff that fulfills why you exist. When you're clear on your personal why, you're able to chart a course and find meaning in what you do. Knowing your purpose, knowing your why, provides meaning for your life. It makes you happy on both a conscious and subconscious level. Your conscious mind likes the logic of doing things with a purpose. Your subconscious mind likes the feeling that purpose gives you.

In *The Purpose Driven Life* (2002), Rick Warren describes to Christians the five purposes God has for people in life. According to Wikipedia, by 2019, the book had sold over thirty-two million copies in eighty-five languages. You may or may not be a Christian, but obviously a lot of people are looking for purpose in their lives. This isn't just a spiritual consideration either. In *Life on Purpose*, the author, a professor at the University of Michigan School of Public Health, points to the health benefits and increased happiness that result from knowing your purpose (Strecher 2016). Knowing your purpose—your personal why—is beneficial to your spiritual, physical, and emotional well-being.

More and more articles, workshops, and books talk about mindfulness. Mindfulness gurus encourage you to focus attention on the present moment without judgement. If you're using all your energy applying your conditioning to getting stuff done, you may actually want to judge that this isn't the best thing for you and then do something about it.

If you know your why, you're in a better position to be present in any given moment. Once you know why you're doing stuff, then it's safe to set aside judgement since you know why you're doing whatever you're doing. Later in the book, when we talk about values, you'll understand the significance of being clear on your personal why and on how that relates to your personal values.

Remember, if you don't know your why, you're not alone. Don't judge yourself or others for not knowing why. Now that you know how important this is, just identify your why. Until you give yourself permission to find your purpose, you're unlikely to discover your why. This is a common problem. Unless your parents, friends, or boss figured out that this knowledge is so important to every aspect of life, they're probably in the same boat as you. You probably don't find a lot of comfort in sharing that particular boat with anyone, but it's a normal situation. The good news is that you're in control of getting out of that boat and discovering your personal why.

CHAPTER 3

Defining Personal Values

What I Do Makes Me Feel Bad, So Why Do I Do It?

All the times that I knew that I was being an ass actually did make me feel bad. What was I to do, though? I had stuff to get done. Leaders lead, and being an ass from time to time comes with the territory, right? I didn't think that it was okay to worry about how I felt if I was getting results. I really didn't want to act like an ass or to be seen as one by the people around me. I felt like I had no choice: that was the problem. Accomplishing what I felt needed to be done was so important to me that I was willing to be an ass and then feel bad about it. I thought that this was just the price a leader must pay. I told myself that how I felt didn't matter because it was all about getting things done. If my feelings didn't matter, it seemed logical to believe that other people's feelings didn't matter either—if we got stuff done, that was all that mattered. Everyone knows that this is how things work, don't they? I'm sure you can see how my conditioning boxed me in, and why this limited perspective made my negative behavior seem to be the only logical option if I was to continue to get things done.

I was trapped. I saw myself as a leader, and getting things done was very important to me. Results at any cost seemed to be how the world worked. I had built a personal value around "Lead, follow, or get out of the way." I had also built a personal value that basically said that my worth as a person was based on getting things done.

I'm a double extrovert—that is, the top two things for me are to get things done and to engage others to get things done. I'll always have that personality, but I've discovered positive ways to get results and to engage other people. Prior to making this discovery, I always wanted to get things done while engaging others in a positive way, but I made getting things done a priority over engaging others if I didn't feel that they were following as they should.

I was raised to believe that hard work is a virtue. I felt that hard work without getting things done was pointless. When I was caught in this trap, I didn't realize that I'd narrowed my personal values and my self-worth to this limited perception of leadership and measuring success on nothing but results. It was a false dichotomy that had become my reality. I felt it was important to step up and lead. Be an ass if I had to be. Get stuff done. Accomplish the goal even if it made me feel bad and left those around me wondering why I was being such an ass. This attitude was at the center of my personal values and it drove my behavior.

When I was in the Army, I was promoted pretty quickly. (Like I said before: being an ass seemed to be okay as long as you got results.) I was a squad leader, but I still lived in the barracks with my troops. One evening, one of the guys had a few beers and felt like joking around. He said, "The cool, the frosty, the frigid, Sergeant Freeze!" He was directing this at me. After he said it, I think he thought I might chill him. He apologized for his joke. I asked him why he called me Sergeant Freeze. He told me that a lot of the guys called me that behind my back. When I asked him why, he told me that no matter what came up in a soldier's life, I'd tell the soldier what to do about it and then tell them to get back to work. He said, "You know, one of the guys tells you that the reason that he was late reporting was that his wife left him and took the kids, the dog, and the car, and moved to her mom's house in another state. You tell him he can move back into the barracks and then he won't need a car and he'll be on time." It was a slight exaggeration, but it put a spotlight on my conditioned approach to getting things done and not worrying too much about feelings.

I understand my conditioning and that there's more than one approach to getting things done now. At that time, I had never really thought about my personal values unless someone called me Sergeant Freeze or called me an ass. I knew that I had values, and I thought I was clear on what they were. I felt that everyone had clear values. I assumed that everyone shared my values. Every speech a president made started off with "My fellow Americans!" Didn't all Americans share the same values? If not, they were wrong. (As a young man, I approached things a lot like people do on social media and in politics today; if you don't agree with me, you're evil!)

At that point in my life, if I had been asked what my values were, I wouldn't have said that I felt it was okay to be an ass, that "Lead, follow, or get out of the way" was my values mantra, or that I didn't think about other people's feelings or values all that much. I would probably have said that leading and getting things done were at the top of my values list, and then I would have gotten busy getting things done.

I heard Morris Massey (1976) talk about values and values programming when I was a student. At that time, Massey was the Associate Dean and Professor of Marketing at the University of Colorado at Boulder. I remember him saying, "Who you are is where you were when; when you were values programming." I have come to realize Massey's meaning: where we lived and what we experienced during childhood (up to around age twelve) forms our values, and that programming is a foundational part of who we are for the rest of our lives. Of course, at the time I didn't understand the significance of this statement to all the things in this book. Massey was a marketing professor, so he must be talking about how values affect people's buying habits. I thought this was noteworthy as a future businessperson, so I made note of it.

I was unaware of how my subconscious mind used feelings to create stories. I didn't understand that these subconscious feelings-generated stories shaped my values programming. I assumed that it was all a very logical process where my conscious mind observed things that would work for me and things that would not work for me. Sorting things that work from things that don't work, building a nice set of values around hard work, and getting things done really made sense to me. Having things make sense lined up nicely with my conditioning. My view of my conditioning was based on the belief that my conscious mind had to agree that the conditioned behavior made sense. For something to make sense, it had to be about getting things done, not much else. Remember, I didn't think I had a choice. At this time, I had allowed my conditioning and values programming to lock me into a fixed mindset. It was years before I first heard about fixed and growth mindsets. By the time I did, I had spent many years in a fixed mindset and had finally moved into a growth mindset as a result of identifying my why, strengths, and values.

The psychologist B.F. Skinner was a pioneer in the field of behaviorism. Skinner didn't believe that humans possess free will. He thought humans respond like Pavlov's dogs, and that's the whole story. I studied Skinner and what he said didn't feel right, but despite my feelings, I had bought into it almost completely. How it felt was irrelevant. If it worked and made sense, that was good enough for me. If dogs would salivate based on conditioning and people would follow based on conditioning, things should go smoothly.

As I matured and noticed effective and even great leaders, my limited, fixed mindset and perspective began making less sense. I observed these leaders getting a lot more done than I did and they never seemed to find it necessary to resort to being asses.

As long as I ignored my innate strengths, never thought about my personal why, and accepted that my values were handed to me for logical review and acceptance, I got things done. There were times when I became frustrated with the performance or level of commitment that I saw from other people, so I would decide it was easier to just do whatever it was myself.

I began wondering if I was as great a leader as I had thought I was. Leadership is about getting other people to do things, not about doing everything yourself. I discovered another problem to add to my confusion over my style of leadership: my observation of leaders who never seemed to need to play the be-an-ass card got great results and people were attracted to them; also, I realized that from time to time people would actually get out of the way rather than follow me.

I was causing an environment where people who worked for me could rationalize their low levels of engagement: I didn't make people feel valued and appreciated, and they knew I'd do their job for them sooner or later. The situation was of my creation.

What Are Values?

Your values are what guide you at the gut level. Values connect subconscious feelings and fundamental beliefs. Those fundamental beliefs are the stuff that is built into us during, what Massey called, values programming. Your values programming was pretty much locked in at around age twelve. For your values to change after that, it requires what Massey called a significant emotional event. Once stuff is mapped into your subconscious, you may need a qualified coach to help you redraw that map.

I was being an ass. It didn't feel good, but I kept being an ass because I thought I had to be that way. It didn't feel good because I was actually experiencing a conflict between my conditioning and values. My conditioning told me that I needed to lead and to get things done no matter what.

Deep down I had a need to be liked. I really wanted to be the kind of person who never acted like an ass. I was observing people that I admired because they got things done *and* they were likeable, approachable, and kind. Unlike B.F. Skinner, I believe that people do have free will.

We choose what feels good and we choose the rationale that we use to make our conscious mind think that we are oh-so-logical. We have the potential to attain and maintain a high level of personal performance by leveraging our why, strengths, and values. Anyone can choose to be effective as well as likeable, approachable, and kind.

You may have had a boss or been around people who talk about shared values. They may have emphasized the importance of the team valuing what they value. When values are really shared, that is powerful stuff (we'll talk about that in the next chapter about organizational values). However, when you listen to the rhetoric about shared values, do you sometimes get the impression that the speaker wants you to figure out his or her values and then line up with those? Does it feel like you're being asked to pretend to be excited about them, saying, "I'll lead, you follow, or get out of the way"?

What Are Your Values?

If you've never considered your personal values, it doesn't mean you don't have personal values—it means that your values aren't clear and well defined in your conscious mind. They affect your subconscious and your feelings all the time. As conditioning moves you away from your innate strengths into behaviors that are far different from your true self, you will experience more stress. When your personal values aren't clear and being honored, stress increases. These stressors may cause your conscious mind to rationalize behaviors that are actually in conflict with your personal values. If you feel a lot of stress or dread going to work, it just might be that your values are trying to get your attention.

Do you wonder how multinational corporations end up doing things that are illegal and cause outrage and even legal action once they're exposed? Perhaps this is the result of people trading their why and values for getting stuff done and being "successful."

Do My Values Matter?

I hope it's obvious that your values matter. If you work for a multinational corporation that is about to lie to the world about the safety or effectiveness of its product, will you look away and cash your bonus check or will you become a whistleblower?

Having a clear awareness of your personal values makes it possible for you to leverage both your innate and conditioned strengths. It might help you to sleep at night and even to keep you out of jail. Your personal values add standards of behavior to your personal why. Your values provide socially acceptable boundaries to the expression of your why.

A why without values can lead to negative expression of that why. Part of my why has always been about leading and getting results. Without clear values, I couldn't get results without being an ass at times; my lack of awareness limited my ability to be results oriented while leading in a positive way.

CHAPTER 4

Understanding Organizational Why, Strengths, and Values

What Did They Expect?

It would be great if this has never happened to you, but if it has, you'll remember exactly how it feels: on more than one occasion I took a job that seemed great. Soon after I started the job, it began to feel like a big mistake. As I recall these situations, it seems that the story played out pretty much the same way in each case.

Each time the interviews were a review of my resume and some get-to-know-you chit-chat. There may have been a couple of "Describe a time when . . ." interview questions. Once this review was out of the way, the interview felt more like a sales pitch. The interviewer talked about how the job was a great opportunity. I found myself getting caught up in the pitch. I got excited about this amazing opportunity. I didn't think at the time to ask some substantive questions, to figure out if this opportunity was right for me based on my personal why, strengths, and values. I couldn't have asked the right questions anyway since I hadn't really identified my why, strengths, and values.

There was no exploration of my personal why, strengths, and values. The people making the hiring decision didn't discover anything about what actually made me tick. I didn't learn anything about the organization's why, strengths, or values either. None of us discovered anything to help identify a culture fit. It was my responsibility to ask questions that would give me insight into the organizations why, strengths, and values. I didn't understand this at the time. Since I didn't know how important this was, asking questions to learn about the company culture never occurred to me. I suspect the interviewers had no idea what their personal and organizational why, strengths, and values were anyway. Besides, since I didn't have a clear picture of my personal why, strengths, and values, I wouldn't have known how to evaluate the organization's culture to see whether this job and I were a good fit.

Over time I found myself less excited about each of these jobs. I also felt that my boss was less excited about me. Too often I found myself doing work that I was conditioned to do but had no real excitement about. I was working hard. I got things done. Sometimes I was an ass. What did they expect? They didn't know. What did I expect? I didn't know either.

More often than I care to remember it felt like I wasn't given the secret to success. I didn't understand that I was given exactly what everybody else in that organization was given. We were all looking at our job descriptions, what we thought our bosses wanted, perhaps even reading the strategic plan document if there was such a thing. No one could identify the organizations why, strengths, and values since that hadn't been worked out. Based on this reality, even if any of us had known our personal why, strengths, and values, the organizations culture would likely have been challenging. For years there have been studies and reports addressing employee engagement levels. Over decades the Gallup organization has tracked the levels of employee engagement. Engaged employees comprise around 30 percent of the workforce with 50 percent disengaged, and the remaining 20 percent is defined as *actively disengaged* (Harter 2018). Actively disengaged employees are undermining the efforts of engaged workers. They make their unhappiness known and may seek opportunities to sabotage the organization

There were times when it seemed that there were situations where I was actually punished for working really hard. I'd like to think I was a victim of actively disengaged coworkers who were undermining my efforts. At times this was probably the case. I didn't know about this range of employee engagement, so I really have no idea what impact that had on me or on the organizations that I worked for. However, I did wonder what I was missing. Why would an organization hire me and not tell me what to do to be a high-performance contributor? Why would someone hire me and then not want me to be all that I could be?

I mention the Gallup data on employee engagement to point out that disengagement is, at least in part, a symptom of fuzzy or nonexistent whys, strengths, and values on the part of employees and their employers.

This reminds me of an experience that I had working in my only fast-food job. I was in high school and it was my first job. Employees were expected to be busy all the time. If it was quiet, we were supposed to clean the dining room and do other preparation and cleaning tasks. We were also expected to be at the cash register to take orders as soon as a customer came in. One day I was mopping the dining room when a customer walked in. We weren't allowed to leave mops and buckets in the dining room, so I wheeled them to the back as I let the customer know that I would be right with them. I took the order, got them their food, and thought everything was fine. As soon as they left, the manager walked out from the back and chewed me out for "looking busy" rather than being where I needed to be to serve customers. He told me that I was good at looking busy rather than really working. I was confused. If I wanted to look busy, I'd choose something easier than swinging a big rag mop!

What did the manager expect from me? At the time it felt like there was some secret to pleasing the boss that I just hadn't figured out. Now I see that situation and situations like it differently. The manager didn't have secret expectations. If I had been bold enough to ask for answers, I suspect he would have felt threatened and fired me. His conditioning led him to believe that chewing people out kept them on their toes and would motivate them to work harder.

Years later, after I started working to develop strategic plans with my clients, I discovered a deeper problem. The problem that I had faced at the jobs I just described was that I didn't have a clear picture of my why, strengths, and values. My bosses didn't either. The deeper problem was that the company that we worked for didn't really know either.

How could I suggest that no one in an organization knew the why, strengths, or values of their business? The evidence is in what many organizations call their strategic plan. Too many organizations don't have a process to create a strategic plan or they write one and never update it. If there's an annual update, a lot of the documents are tactical implementation plans without any strategic focus. Tactical plans are important, but without strategic plans built on the why, strengths, and values of the organization, they are hard work without clear focus.

When business leaders say that they have done their strategic planning, I like to ask them to describe what the plan is focused on. What they describe can often be rephrased as "build stuff, sell stuff." If that's your organizations strategic plan, you don't have a strategic plan. Everybody is in business to sell something to someone. Even nonprofits are selling their services to someone and selling someone else on the idea that it's good to contribute to their cause. There's no market differentiation in this. Worse, there's nothing to inspire people to join the team and to contribute all that they have. This results in burnout, job hopping, and a host of other problems that plague organizations. Remember the Gallup engagement data? It's tough to give your all to an organization that doesn't communicate a meaningful vision. High-performance organizations are the ones that have figured this out and done the work to know their why, strengths, and values. These high-performance organizations also have clear written strategic and tactical implementation plans that the entire team understands.

Punished for Working Really Hard

Have you ever been in a situation where you felt like you were being punished for working really hard? You put in long hours; you meet deadlines; you sacrifice what you want to do and do what you think is expected—then you get passed over for promotion and receive lower scores on your performance review than you feel you deserve. As a business owner, this might look like bidding for jobs and seeing your competition winning work that you felt you deserved or seeing your best people go to work for the competition for a small salary increase.

You've probably experienced this sort of thing at some point in your career. You may be experiencing it now. It's possible that you're less gifted or don't work as hard as you think you do. It's also possible that you're working really hard on stuff that nobody really cares about. You should ask yourself whether you know how you're work contributes to the strategic plan of the organization. As a business owner, it may be that your business isn't inspiring employees to stay or prospective customers to do business with you. If "build stuff, sell stuff" is all you've got to offer, employees may see you as a steppingstone and customers are likely to see you as a commodity provider. If that's the case, price is the only differentiator. You're also a commodity if you're just another warm body chasing a paycheck. Commodities aren't valued: they're bought at the lowest possible price and are often replaceable with a commodity from another provider.

Do You Want Out?

I coached a chief operations officer who was referred to me by his CEO. The CEO wanted me to work with him because of challenges between this individual and the staff, vendors, and customers. She felt that he was so good at what he did that it would be better to invest in coaching him to be a better team player than to replace him. When we first met, he shared his frustration over how the employees failed to do their jobs, constantly forcing him to clean up after them. Second, he described vendors who never got orders right. Third, he felt that the customers were always changing what they wanted, were never satisfied, and he had to deal with their unreasonable demands while he was cleaning up everyone else's messes.

His view of everyone around him reminded me of something that a close friend would often say. Whenever she was thinking about changing jobs, getting a divorce, moving to another state, or whatever, she would say, "But wherever I go, I'm there!"

I shared her story with the client. He looked like he was about to punch me. Then he said, "You're saying that I'm the problem!" I told him, "I'm saying that you're the common denominator in everything that you've shared." He said, "You're right. I am the problem." This was the first step needed to move forward. He had to own his part in these situations before we could work out a plan to help him have a more effective approach to all the things that frustrated him and led to his CEO hiring me to work with him.

If you want out of whatever situation you're in, getting out may be appropriate. There are times that call for a job change, divorce, move, or whatever. However, you'll make better decisions about making changes when you do the work to define your why, strengths, and values first. If you own a business and you want out of your own company, you may feel trapped. The good news is that you can change the situation to shape your experiences in order to feel fully engaged with your own company. I share this because I've met too many business owners and executives who are miserable. They often say, "I really can't complain, but . . ." These folks know that others envy their success and accomplishments, but they're putting out a huge amount of effort and aren't feeling that it's really worth it. Your life really can be a lot more than just making a living.

That's Not Cool versus That's Amazing

If you work for, or own, a business that lacks a true strategic plan—a business where "build stuff, sell stuff" is the plan—it's time for a change. It's never too late to define your organizations why, strengths, and values. Once you have that done, then you're in a much better position to craft a meaningful strategic plan that will produce significant results. As Morris Massey informed us, values don't change without significant emotional events. Your why may change as a result of personal growth, changing opportunities, or other factors. Your conditioned strengths change constantly as you learn new things. Just as strategic planning should be done annually, it's a really good idea to revisit and update your why, strengths, and values regularly.

Working for someone like that client I coached isn't cool. Being that client isn't cool either. You may have noticed that a lot of my story in this book is about how I acted like an ass. That client was described as an ass by some of those who had to work with him. Like me, he didn't know how to get stuff done without being an ass. Feeling stuck, just working for your paycheck, wondering if what you're experiencing is all that there is, are all negative places that can be escaped once you know why you want something different. Discovering your why will help you define your innate and conditioned strengths. This discovery will equip you with the tools to change your situation. Living true to your values provides you with the ability to use your strengths to pursue your why in a positive and sustainable way. Figuring out that there are options and that you have the power to change is amazing.

CHAPTER 5

Aligning Personal and Organizational Why, Strengths, and Values

I Was in the Wrong Place

Looking back on jobs that I've had where acting the ass seemed okay, where I was working hard but felt like I was punished for it, where the company was unaware of its why, strengths, and values, I felt like was in the wrong place. They may have been the wrong organizations or it may have had a lot more to do with me. Before I clarified my why, strengths, and values, I was in the wrong place mentally and emotionally.

When I graduated from high school, a friend of my grandmother's told me to grab any balloon that was going up. That made sense. It's not bad advice if you can identify the balloons that will support your goals and your why, strengths, and values. When I grabbed at any balloon that drifted past, I failed to assess the ability of that balloon (job) to fulfill my career goals *and* my mental and emotional needs. Knowing your why, strengths, and values provides you with awareness of your mental and emotional needs, because these core concepts are what defines clarity in your conscious and subconscious self. When people talk about being self-aware, they mean personal clarity in these three concepts. Often, I was excited to take a job only to discover that it wasn't what I had hoped it was like—I had grabbed a pretty little balloon only to discover that it couldn't lift me up; instead, it let me down.

To make matters worse, the people who hired me were disappointed that that little balloon and I drifted down. They didn't know the weight of my mental and emotional needs, so they assumed their little balloon was going to be just great at lifting me higher and higher while they reaped the benefit of having me on their team.

I'm not saying that I didn't experience success throughout my career. I was successful when measured against my peers. But, keep in mind that I'm looking back through the lens of knowing the extent of low-level engagement in most workplaces. In addition, knowing how much of my potential wasn't being used, because I'd allowed my conditioning to restrict what tools I used, gave me a new perspective on the gap between my success and my potential for greater accomplishment.

People who can sustain high-performance know their why, strengths, and values.

Do You Have to Compromise Everything to Succeed?

At the end of the 2005 movie *Fun with Dick and Jane*, the credits include a special thanks to former Enron CEO Kenneth Lay, other Enron employees, Tyco, WorldCom, and other companies that stole employee pensions then filed for bankruptcy. The movie is a comedy about the CEO, Jack McCallister (played by Alec Baldwin), and his fall guy, Dick Harper (played by Jim Carrey). Jack sets Dick up to face the media and jail when Jack cashes out all the company's money. Enron, Tyco, and others are thanked because they actually robbed their employees and shareholders. It's a funny story unless you've counted on a company only to have them rob you. The feeling that employees have robbed business owners isn't funny either. In both cases, values have been ignored in the pursuit of a short-term gain.

The Enron scandal was way back in 2001. In 2002 the Sarbanes-Oxley Act, also known as the Public Company Accounting Reform and Investor Protection Act, was enacted in the United States to protect us all from a similar incident. At last, steps were taken to assure that corporations couldn't take advantage of unsuspecting people.

In September 2015, news outlets started reporting that the U.S. Environmental Protection Agency had discovered software that Volkswagen had installed in their diesel automobiles to cheat on diesel engine emissions measurements. On December 4, 2019, a *Car and Driver* magazine reporter, Clifford Atiyeh, wrote that Volkswagen had installed the cheating software in 500,000 diesel cars in the U.S. and in about 10.5 million more worldwide.

I'm not an attorney or a CPA, but I suspect the Sarbanes-Oxley Act wasn't helpful in addressing this new global corporate scam since Volkswagen found a different way to cheat people. It seems that it's not possible to make enough rules, or to monitor organizations closely enough, to guarantee that this unthinkable behavior stops. Of course, Volkswagen did face fines and penalties. The point is that rules and regulations don't stop bad behavior. Ignoring values that create positive culture and protect people creates corporate cultures where people repeatedly come up with schemes for short-term gain and where, somehow, robbing the public becomes thinkable.

Whenever we hear about stuff like this, we're outraged. You may ask yourself how this can keep happening. When people aren't clear on their values and organizations haven't worked to define their values, it becomes easy to justify bad behavior. Even bad behavior on a global scale can be justified by rationalizations that we use in our personal lives when we want to take an easier path than the path we innately know is right. We tell ourselves things like "Everyone does it," "This won't hurt anyone," "We have to do this to be competitive," and "I have to get this done, no matter what." Amazingly, people jump into schemes, like Enron and Volkswagen, without questioning one another or themselves.

Why aren't corporate values in place that prevent this sort of thing? Why do executives and their employees keep doing stuff like this? I suggest that it's a dangerous situation that a lot of organizations and teams are in, organizations and teams that haven't been intentional about developing and discussing the why, strengths, and values of the organization and about how to attract people with personal why, strength, and values that fit the organization. When people in positions of leadership don't talk about values, we assume that our personal feelings are supposed to be left at home, that we're in jeopardy of doing things that are getting done in ways that would be unacceptable if we were clear on our values.

Why You're Exhausted

Do you remember the metaphorical twenty-pound sledgehammer we talked about in the first chapter? Picture yourself going through your day carrying a twenty-pound sledgehammer. Now, consider items to represent other aspects of your self-image. Let's add a bag of golf clubs and a filled hiking pack to represent the recreational side of you, a vacuum cleaner and household cleaning items to represent your responsible homemaker side, and a car seat and some kids toys if you're a parent; while we're at it, let's think about other heavy tools to represent the stuff that you do at work. Are you beginning to see why you're tired? Most of us carry a lot of stuff around with us everywhere. When you're not clear on who you are and you don't know your why, you can't ever be sure when it's okay to put anything down. This picture is of your mental and emotional world if you could see how you carry a confused collection of your conditioning and innate stuff around. The worst part of this is, you may even be carrying all this to bed with you. If you're like me, you don't want to sleep with any of the stuff that I just listed. This night and day burden is why you're exhausted.

To make matters worse, if you're ignoring deeply buried values, those are probably stressing you more than you realize. If you're behaving in ways that conflict with your values programming, it will affect you and may be robbing you of sleep.

It Just Got Easy!

Now picture a garage with a workshop area and nice professionally organized storage (not the piles to climb over that a lot of garages have in them). Now picture that you're clear on which of your strengths are conditioned and which are innate. You have all your conditioned tools in their place in one toolbox. Your innate strengths are the tools in another toolbox. The golf clubs and backpacks are on the shelves. The car seats are in the car. Toys are inside in the kid's toy box. The cleaning stuff is either where you want to keep it or the cleaning service brings it with them when they clean your house. You know exactly what you've got. You know exactly where everything is. You know exactly when and how to use it. Now when you climb into bed, none of that stuff is there with you—you'll sleep better. I bet you're feeling less exhausted already.

Picture yourself at work with this same level of clarity. Your organization is as clear and organized as you. Are you feeling like a whole new high-performance player? If you aren't, it's probably because negative self-talk is whispering in your ear. Negative self-talk is built by behavioral conditioning that is overly critical or by strong conditioning that takes you away from being connected to your true self, both of which create internal conflict. That sort of conditioning burdens you with carrying your conditioned tools around and makes you feel that working really hard and being exhausted is how life has to be.

This book is titled *Engage! How to Attract and Inspire a High-Performance Team* specifically because I have helped many people who were stuck: people who didn't have any idea what their why, strengths, and values were. I have seen the transformation in these people as we got rid of the negative self-talk and conditioning that kept them from moving from exhaustion and burn-out to high-performance. Working with organizations, I've seen whole teams accomplish this as well. I admit that I've also seen situations where some members of a team get it, but the boss was unwilling or unable to change. High-performance teams can't flourish if leaders won't move from thinking that they're totally in control and that everybody needs to just keep working really hard and to put up with him being an ass because that's just how the world works. When all team members know their why, strengths, and values, plus they have clarity on the why, strengths, and values of their organization, individuals are set up to succeed and organizations to thrive—and everyone is engaged. In chapter 6 we will look at the need for understanding the why, strengths, and values of other team members. That's another key to be a high-performance team.

There's a common wisdom in coaching, consulting, and other helping professions: we can only help people who want help. People who are too afraid of change to consider any other way of doing things will continue to do what they've always done and to get what they've always gotten. Unless you and your business are dead, there's always hope. Positive results are available to anyone as soon as they're ready to do the work to discover their why, strengths, and values and to properly use them with fellow team members. We'll explore these interactions in the next couple chapters.

CHAPTER 6

Understanding the Why, Strengths, and Values of Others on the Team

Everything is a Team Sport!

I have talked a lot about the negative aspects of my leadership style before I discovered my personal why, strengths, and values. I was successful even while I was stuck in limiting behavior patterns and lacked clarity around my why, strengths, and values. I've offered you encouragement by sharing that I did finally gain clarity about my personal why, understanding of my innate and conditioned strengths, and my personal values. I also discovered positive and effective behaviors that I already had the potential to use that set me free from being trapped in the belief that there were times when being an ass was the only option. There wasn't a single event or a specific date when I saw the light and turned to more positive behavior. As a member of a lot of teams, I started to see that I had much to learn and that there is more than one way to get stuff done.

In chapter 4 I talked about my manager at the fast-food restaurant. I knew that I didn't want to emulate his approach. When I was in the Army, I noticed that some leaders got a lot done without having to act like asses. These exceptional leaders got results from their troops. They also got respect and loyalty from their teams. They understood that they needed each of their people to accomplish their mission. They were aware of the role that each person played on their team and they supported their people to be the best that they could be at fulfilling their individual roles. This was my first realization of the team-sport side of getting stuff done. Great leaders engage their people and inspire them to be the best that they can be.

Years after I left the Army, I was in sales at a technology company that built data networks and communications systems for large enterprises and for communications carriers. We sold very expensive, very complex technology to businesses that had a lot of information to send from place to place. Charlie was our general manager. He was a master at building and inspiring high-performance teams. He understood everything that we did, and he could sell as well as any of us. He often supported our sales efforts without displacing us or diminishing our role as the sales lead with the customer. If customers asked him for ballpark pricing, he always said, "It'll be more than a Corvette and less than a Learjet." This ballpark range was a good description of the cost of our solutions. After a customer spoke with him, he immediately directed the customer back to the sales executive to finalize details and for sales engineering to give the customer a proposal and pricing. In conversation with us, Charlie could ballpark most deals to within $10,000 or $20,000, so it wasn't that he couldn't give a more accurate estimate to customers, it's that he understood and trusted how each of us added to the best outcome for our customers and for the company.

Charlie was also a master at man*agement by wandering around* (MBWA). I was first exposed to the concept when I read *In Search of Excellence: Lessons from America's Best-Run Companies* (1982) written by Thomas J. Peters and Robert H. Waterman Jr. When I saw Charlie at work, I knew that he did what the book was describing. Charlie was almost always available. He often dropped by just when he was needed. He always knew what was going on in any deal that we were working on, and he often had information that we needed just when we needed it. He saved us a lot of time and frustration because we didn't have to chase the information down ourselves. All that said, it never felt like he was micromanaging us. I always felt that we were trusted and valued. His approach felt like the best possible service and support that we could hope to have with strong leadership woven in. By making the effort to understand and support each member of the team, Charlie earned our respect and we felt an obligation to bring our best to everything that we did in response to that support. I used to wonder how Charlie got anything done since he spent so much time wandering around and supporting every part of the organization from sales and engineering to installation and administration. I now understand that he didn't spend much time dealing with drama or dysfunction. The time invested in supporting all of us, inspiring us, and wandering around in fact gave Charlie the time to wander around every day. He knew us and the business better than any manager that I've ever worked with. Since he inspired high performance and he was leading a high-performance team, he could invest his energy and time to create great outcomes rather than be a firefighter who spent his days dealing with problems.

In this chapter, we'll explore the value and importance of understanding the why, strengths, and values of the other people on your team. Charlie is an example of a leader that got this and knew how to develop why, strengths, and values in the team. I don't know how much of his prowess as a leader was conditioned and how much was innate strength. It doesn't matter because each of us can build high-performance teams that function as well as Charlie's team did, even if we never master all that Charlie was able to do. Once you know your why, strengths, and values, and have an awareness of the why, strengths, and values of the other members of your team, you can determine who should handle what in order to sustain high-performance outcomes.

We're all members of multiple teams. Each team has different people who bring different potential to the team. The needs of each team are different. Each team has unique organizational whys, strengths, and values. If you have a job, then you have your work team. You may be involved with nonprofit organizations as a volunteer, running a busy household, or working on a start-up business on the side that's not yet profitable, or all three. There's your family, friends, neighborhood, clubs, faith community, professional organizations, and other places where you interact with others. All of these fit the definition of team in this chapter. Imagine bringing your true self and your full potential to everything that you're involved in. Remember, playing from your innate strengths doesn't feel like work.

Any time a group (two or more people) comes together, they form a team. The question is, How effective is this team? None of us has to try to become Charlie—he was unique. You and everyone else on your teams are unique too. The secret is to do the work to discover your personal why, strengths, and values, to have that information for your organization where possible, and to tune in to the cues that tell you what the whys, strengths, and values the other members of the team are bringing to the party. I'm not gifted like Charlie, but I can team with others and together we can do all that Charlie did. It takes a lot of communication and commitment, but the return on investment is amazing, no matter how you measure it.

I encourage clients to identify their *key performance indicator* (KPI) to measure the return on doing the work to discover the why, strengths, and values for yourself, your organization, and your teammates. Seeing results that are measured by KPI inspires you and your people to continue to put energy and effort into building a high-performance organization. Here are some suggestions of things that can be measured to show the value of this approach to building your team:

- Cost of turnover
  - Lost productivity
  - Recruiting and training new people
  - Lost clients and acquisition cost to replace lost business

- Productivity and engagement
  - Before and after why, strength, and values work
    - quality levels
    - output
    - absenteeism and sick time
    - employee theft/shrinkage
    - workplace injuries
  - New opportunities resulting from teamwork
    - ideas and initiatives brought forth by multiple team members
    - employees initiating improvements that are outside of their job description

- referrals for the business from team members' personal spheres of influence

This is not a complete list. These are just examples. What your KPI looks like will depend on your organizations why, strengths, and values.

Disengaged—What's with the Attitude?

We have already talked about the problem of having around 50 percent of workers in the United States in the disengaged category and around 20 percent of US employees being highly disengaged, leaving only around 30 percent of the workforce in the engaged range. Let's look at these percentages in another way. Less than a third of workers are bringing their A game to their jobs. The rest are doing what they must do to keep their jobs, but they're not giving it their all. Imagine, around 20 percent, or one in five, of the people around you in the average workplace are ducking their responsibilities and may be looking for ways to detract from the team. These people are negative, taking energy away from the team by gossiping, complaining, and obstructing the goals of the team. They may even seek to harm the business.

In chapter 4 we looked at incidents like the actions that led to the passage of the Sarbanes-Oxley Act and the global Volkswagen diesel scandal. A lack of focus on values clearly leads to incidents like these. It's easy to be outraged by things on that scale. Now, consider the employee engagement percentages. If you're a business owner, there's little doubt that having up to 70 percent of your employees fall short of active engagement probably makes you feel outraged. The lack of active engagement may seem personal since it's your business. If you're an employee who's not performing at a level that would be defined as active engagement, you're probably not too proud of yourself either.

The In-Crowd and the Rest

If you're a business owner or CEO, you may have accepted that less than one third of your team will be actively engaged. Let me suggest that resigning yourself to that is like when I believed that I had no choice but to act like an ass.

If you work for someone else, you may rationalize your less than full engagement as well. Perhaps you feel that there's an in-crowd that gets all the perks and that you're giving all that your boss deserves from you. You may even tell yourself that there are natural-born overachievers and that the fully engaged group is a bunch of workaholics or suck-ups. If you focus instead on the joy and energy that comes from discovering your potential and engaging your why, your strengths, and your values to accomplish things that you've never accomplished before, you're catching on to what you get out of this, regardless of what anybody else is doing.

Understanding the Why, Strengths, and Values of Others on the Team

If you don't see how discovering your why, strengths, and values will change you in ways that you will like, please go back and read the earlier chapters again. Unless you're aware of your why, strengths, and values and you're applying them to be all that you can be, you're not living a fulfilling life. Being stuck in anything less than your full potential drains you. You will experience burnout, frustration, and you'll miss out on the joy that you could experience from life.

Anyone who is a leader of an organization owes it to the fully engaged employees and to themselves to clearly define the why, strengths, and values of the organization. Once that's done, communicate it to the whole team: you can expect everyone to up their engagement level. High-performance teams attract high performance. People either engage or move on. Once people experience being part of a high-performance team, they generally want more of it.

There's Hope If We All Lean In

I know an athlete who medaled in the Olympics a couple of times. This high-performance person believes that high-performance teams are very rare. This medalist feels that we should always strive for a high-performance team but that we'll seldom attain that goal and can never sustain it. Once you, your organization, and your teammates are all clear on why, strengths, and values, there's no reason that you can't attain and sustain a high-performance team.

Imagine how uncomfortable it will be for folks who are actively disengaged to stand by while most of the people around them are enjoying the teamwork and satisfaction that comes from being high-performance players on a high-performance team!

CHAPTER 7

Your Personal Alignment

Finally, It All Clicked

After years of seeking ways to improve my leadership abilities and effectiveness, I'd learned a lot. I had seen exceptionally good and shockingly poor leadership. Starting with several exceptional officers and senior NCOs that I served with in the Army, civilian managers of all descriptions, and Charlie (the general manager in the last chapter), each provided me with more understanding of different approaches to getting things done. I worked to apply what I observed effective leaders do, with varying degrees of success.

I tried to avoid emulating negative behaviors and to evaluate my own behavior in order to identify and reduce bad behaviors in myself. I observed that some leaders, like

Charlie, got a lot done without ever resorting to being asses. I focused on developing conditioned behaviors that helped me to be more effective, with more people, more often. These behaviors (tools) made a real difference in producing positive engagements and better outcomes. This was good; however, I found myself experiencing increasing stress levels despite the gains in effectiveness. It was strange: I felt less fulfilled than I'd hoped that I would when I got things done. However, I was able to do more with a wider range of personality types without being an ass as often! I thought that I should feel that life was good. Being stressed a lot of the time robbed me of that life-is-good feeling. I found myself asking if the rewards were worth the stress.

Finally, it all clicked. I read a pile of books and I got coaching support to help me sort out my personal why, my strengths (based on my innate and conditioned behaviors), and my values. With this coaching help, I discovered how to play from my innate behavior strengths (my true self) and how to use conditioned behaviors as the valuable tools that they are.

Your Personal Why

Discovering my personal why led me to start a new career as a coach and consultant. For years I operated as though getting things done and being in charge was my why; however, my why is helping people to discover and develop their potential once they understand their why, strengths, and values, then apply each element to their calling. As I became more self-aware, I realized that I'd always been drawn to situations where I could train, coach, and otherwise develop the people around me. Further, I realized that engaging with an effective team was the most enjoyable thing that I ever did. Once I understood the reason why I behaved in the ways that I did and I was able to separate my conditioned behaviors from my innate behaviors, I could accomplish more than I dreamed without the stress that I'd been carrying around. Your why defines the basic energy that drives everything in your life—this is the reason that I have talked about discovering your personal why throughout this book.

Your Personal Strengths

We've talked a lot about personal strengths. Innate and conditioned behaviors can be strengths or weaknesses. The value of a behavior depends on how clear you are on all of your behaviors and what triggers a given behavior. With that clarity you're able to manage your behaviors as tools that are strengths. Without clarity, you, like Pavlov's dogs, may be triggered when someone rings a bell (pushes your buttons) and you react.

When I'm working with clients. I talk about the buttons that others have identified in the person that I'm working with. Those buttons, like the bell, are the stimulus that elicits a behavior in you. When you haven't done the work to understand your own behaviors and what may elicit different behaviors, you might feel that others are always pushing your buttons. You might not feel that you have control over your own behavior, or at least, over your feelings in that moment. Keep in mind, your behaviors and responses are all that you really can control. The clearer you are on this the more positive and stronger your behaviors can be.

You don't control how other people react or behave. At times others may intentionally push your buttons to manipulate you. At other times, your response has little if anything to do with the situation or the other person. When your buttons are based on past experiences, people may bump into buttons that they didn't intend to press. Have you ever had a situation where you felt that someone was trying to upset you or get a reaction out of you? Once you reacted, did they react to your behavior in a way that surprised you? This is an example of your lack of self-awareness (and probably the same issue for the other person) causing an escalation of reaction. Imagine how much workplace drama stems from two people who haven't done the work to understand their own behaviors (and buttons), who unintentionally push buttons.

Your Personal Values

Characters with conflicted values and tortured by moral ambiguity are common in graphic novels and popular movies. However, failing to develop clear definitions of your personal values and to live according to your values is at best stressful and unrewarding and at worst potentially a path to finding yourself looking back wondering how your life ended up compromised and empty.

Align with Your Teammates and Organizational Why, Strengths, and Values

Once you know your why, strengths, and values and you know how each applies to your organization, things can become very rewarding. As you communicate what matters to you and expose your true self, you begin to create a safe place for others to do the same. If you're part of an organization that supports this and has done the work to provide clarity around the organizational why, strengths, and values, you and your teammates will discover more and more ways that the alignments between and among the people on the team will reveal opportunities and will make you an increasingly effective high-performance team.

An aspect of these alignments is the discovery of your group's collective wisdom. *Collective wisdom*, or collective intelligence, has been proven to yield better results than one person in a group can produce alone (Landemore and Elster 2012; Leimeister 2010). A significant benefit of full engagement from the whole team is that the whole group gains input from more eyes, ears, and brains, all focused on shared outcomes and on the best solutions to problems. When this happens, it also shifts the leadership focus to the group dynamic. This shift is beneficial since the group dynamic is what defines your culture.

CHAPTER 8

Establishing and Maintaining Clear Communication and a Culture That Nurtures High-Performance

But Can We Sustain This?

It's unlikely that you can sustain a high-performance team by force of will, no matter how charismatic, eloquent, or inspirational you are. However, leveraging teamwork makes it very possible to attain and sustain a high-performance team.

Ducks, geese, and other migratory birds fly in a V formation known as a *skein*. The reason is that the birds take turns flying at the front of the V. Whichever bird is in lead position is working harder than the rest. The lead bird helps all the following birds because the followers benefit from flying in the updraft created by the wingtip vortices of the lead bird. This updraft benefits every bird except the leader. When the lead bird needs a break, another takes the lead position and the flock continues its journey.

In the military, "taking point" places the point person in greater danger than the rest of the team. When someone has taken point, they're the first to discover the minefields and are first to face the oncoming enemy forces. The ranking person is not generally the one on point; it's a very important position, but it's not always the ideal spot for the leader because the leader can't supervise the troops and direct activities other than navigation and watching for the enemy. If you have taken point, or are on point, you have to maintain a heightened awareness and be hypervigilant for the sake of yourself and your entire unit. You know that you're a trusted and valued part of the team since everyone is depending on you to get them where they need to go without stepping on a mine or being caught in an ambush. In the Army, we would rotate the person who was on point. Heightened awareness and hypervigilance are exhausting after a while, and it's important to have someone who's fresh in this vitally important position.

I have heard people say that you can't sustain a high-performance team (such as the athlete that I mentioned in chapter 6). I disagree with this premise. Just as migratory birds work together to reduce the amount of energy that is needed to make remarkably long flights, people can work together to maintain a high level of performance. Just as military units change up the person that is on point to assure that the point person is fresh and able to maintain heightened awareness and hypervigilance, we can leverage the members of our team to support the whole team. Encouraging different team members to take point from time to time benefits everyone. If more than one person on the team has a heightened awareness of situations and objectives and is hypervigilant in looking for opportunities, this increases your potential to identify and capitalize on things that might otherwise have been missed. When multiple people are looking for ways to leverage your organizational strengths, you will discover more opportunities and be able to leverage organizational strengths to more fully realize your team's potential. By sharing leadership and point responsibilities, it's possible to maintain a level of team performance that is high and can be maintained indefinitely.

We've talked about allowing different members of your team to take point at different times. This only makes sense if you know the strengths of the people put on point. For example, if the situation calls for a focus on financial considerations, you'll probably pick a different person for point than you would if it was a sales driven situation. Knowing the strengths of the people on your team helps to identify the best resource for each situation. If you're the boss, understanding and accepting that there may be times that someone other than you is the best person to be on point for something shows your team that you value them and appreciate their strengths. By the way, if you're not the strongest person in any given area, chances are everyone on the team already knows this and will respect that you're wise and humble enough to admit it. This approach assures that the best equipped person is in the lead position for whatever the team is working on at any given time. By doing this, the team can leverage all the talent and brain power on the team. Switching up the person who is on point also energizes the whole group because everyone knows that they're valued and that they're being challenged, so they feel that they're making a real contribution to the team. This stands in sharp contrast to the hierarchical model where people become disengaged, bosses burn out, team potential is not leveraged, and opportunities are missed.

I'm not suggesting that you throw out the org chart and turn everybody loose to do whatever they like, nor am I suggesting that it's beneficial to fail to hold people accountable; the opposite is true. When what I suggest is implemented in your organization, the people on your team will be very clear on who is best at doing particular things: they will know who is on point at any given time and what is expected of them. This is only true if your team has all the why, strengths, and values awareness nailed and is communicating effectively. The team must have clear, well defined goals and know its desired outcomes. People perform best when they have a very clear, well defined understanding of their role on the team and how what they do contributes to those well-defined goals of the organization. High-performance teams are structured and do a lot of planning. By being open to switching up the point person and to looking to everybody on the team to step up as leaders, it provides the benefit of having everybody on the team prepared and able to offer updraft to empower others, to bring their brains to work, to know that they can make a difference, and to be engaged.

Sustainable, high-performance teams must have high-trust, high-communication leadership. This requires that the leader be self-aware and in tune with the why, strengths, and values of themselves, the organization, and their team. This is very different from micromanaging the people that you lead. It involves being someone that inspires people, values people, provides others with opportunity, and views others as valuable and important as individuals, not just as resources to be exploited for personal gain.

So, You Think You're Communicating

In chapter 7 I talked briefly about the drama that can result when your buttons are pushed and when your reaction pushes someone else's buttons. That's an example of ineffective communication. Back when I was unclear on my why, strengths, and values, I was aware of times that others felt that I was being an ass. It didn't occur to me that I may have made the situation worse by being unclear in my communication. If engaged people aren't doing what you expect, it's likely that you didn't communicate as clearly as you thought.

The following is an example of poor communication in an organizational setting. The client was a family owned business that had been founded in the 1800s. The CEO was a fifth-generation descendant of the founder. The business had locations throughout the US, and the senior management was almost all family members. When I first met with the CEO, he was concerned that the business might go under on his watch. Imagine the pressure that he must have felt! I interviewed him about their current situation and the reason for his concerns. He felt that they had a very cohesive senior management group and that everyone was on the same page. Their strategic plan boiled down to "build stuff, sell stuff." The company's revenues were flat, and he saw more and more competition in a space that his company had dominated for over one hundred years. He agreed to let me survey the senior management to identify how each answered a series of questions about the vision, strategic direction, and alignment of these elements for the management group. Each of them responded with answers that provided a lot of information about what was happening in their region or department. It seemed that the whole group thought that all the other managers saw the operations pretty much as they did. The CEO was shocked. I suggested that he bring the managers in for a two-day meeting to do what I call *goal focusing*. The plan

Establishing and Maintaining Clear Communication and a Culture That Nurtures High-Performance

was to have me facilitate a strategic planning session that would give the managers the opportunity to provide input on, and to buy in to, a plan that they all agreed with and could communicate to their regions and departments. We completed that process and established this as an approach that has served that company well for over twenty years.

The CEO and the other senior management thought that they were communicating. The problem was that they were assuming that everybody else agreed with what they were doing because nobody said anything to indicate otherwise. Each senior manager was so busy running their own area that they really didn't take time to think about other areas. The CEO had the foresight to recognize that flat revenue and increased competition would eventually cause decreasing revenues and potential failure for the business. They discovered that communication must be intentional and that assumptions about the effectiveness of their communication may be wrong and should be verified.

High-performance teams are high-communication teams. I have worked with senior managers who felt that they had to "overcommunicate" to get people to understand what they were saying. Effective communication isn't overcommunication: it's a process where the message sender verifies that they have been understood and where the message receiver verifies that what they think they've been told is what the sender intended. It's a process where everybody is responsible for assuring effective communications. Years ago I discovered a very simple model for direct communication. I can't find any reference to it so I can't give credit to the person who came up with it. It's the AIR Model: *A* stands for *attend*, *I* stands for *investigate*, and *R* stands for *respond*. Attending suggests an attentive, active engagement with more focus than most of us usually give to listening. Investigating is the step that follows attending and requires verification of one's understanding of the message. The attending and investigating continues between the message sender and receiver until both agree that the intended communication was received. Once *A* and *I* are accomplished, the receiver is in a good position to respond. Responding may be giving the original message sender additional information or it may be acting in response to the message. The beauty of AIR is that using this active listening model avoids reaction in place of response. It may take more time to approach communication this way, but it actually avoids miscommunications that take time and potentially money as well as reducing the drama that tends to result when someone reacts to a communication.

That Isn't What You Expected?

When organizational leaders delegate tasks, they may think that they're empowering their people. If you give someone a task, do you also give them step-by-step instructions on how you want them to do the task? There are obvious examples of situations that require adherence to a step-by-step process such as in manufacturing, chemical operations, and regulatory compliance rules. However, many workplace situations allow for flexibility and creativity.

Empowering people to use their strengths to come up with a plan for getting the assigned results increases engagement and may reveal better approaches that would otherwise have been missed. People tend to resent being told how to do every step of a task unless they are being trained or the task is a step-by-step process. If you can step back and focus on the outcomes rather than being overly concerned that team members didn't do it the "right" way ("right" referring to your way, rather than the ethical way that aligns with the organizations values), you'll increase your team's engagement.

How You'll Know That You're Effective

True leaders understand that rather than taking a my-way-or-the-highway approach, where others are expected to passively comply with a superior's dictates—whether they understand the rationale for the action—and where they disagree with whatever is being driven forward, leaders instead know that they can accomplish more when people embrace and understand the need for the solution. Lao Tzu, an ancient Chinese philosopher, stated,

> A leader is best when people barely know that he exists, not so good when people obey and acclaim him, worst when they despise him. Fail to honor

people, they fail to honor you. But a good leader, who talks little, when his work is done, his aims fulfilled, they will say, "We did this ourselves." (Lawson and Roy 2015)

If your goal is to achieve what is best, to lead a high-performance team that delivers on your vision, to accomplish revolutionary change that makes a difference in the world, then you may have to trade being center stage and give up some of the ego that drives a my-way-or-the-highway mentality in order to enjoy that best outcome. Significant improvement and revolutionary change requires a high-performance team to deliver on your vision, and they'll only follow you when you're being a true leader and will join you because they agree with your vision, embracing it as their own.

Most people in business say that their first priority is getting results. If this is actually true, then fully engaging the energy and brain power of the people around you, bringing that energy into alignment with the goal (results), and increasing the innovative input that comes from an engaged team—that feels that their input matters and may make a difference (leveraged results)—is the only logical approach to take. If you're one of those my-way-or-the-highway bosses, or if you work for one of these folks, there's an agenda at play that is about something other than getting results. As a business owner or as the boss, you've every right to run your business however you see fit. However,

Establishing and Maintaining Clear Communication and a Culture That Nurtures High-Performance

come clean and realize that you're actually concerned about something other than getting results, or at least concerned about something other than leveraging your resources to increase your chances of getting the best possible results. If you're only interested in the best results that can be attained based on everybody lining up and compliantly doing everything your way, you may want to ask yourself why this is your reality. I'd suggest that bosses who can only allow their own vote to count are afraid. True leaders are fearlessly empowered by their ability to lead themselves, to lead a team, to follow another true leader, and to adjust to changing situations by leveraging all available resources, especially other people. If you're a true leader, you attract people who are passionate about the same thing as you, and your people are working hard because they really want to contribute to the success of the effort and to be part of a high-performance team. When we have people who feel part of something bigger than themselves, who are valuable contributors to a significant and positive outcome, and who are willingly following where we are leading, then what's there to be afraid of? We might be afraid to share the credit for our success with others and to show appreciation for their contributions; however, it's amazing to do that because credit and appreciation increase exponentially in proportion to how much you share them with others.

I talked about key performance indicators (KPI) in chapter 6. If you and your team have well-defined KPI and measure KPI, you know when the team is effective and when it needs to engage the strengths of its members to determine the problems behind issues. The problem might be in communication or in any number of other areas. The good news is, the team is focused on using a high level of engagement to accomplish your outcomes, so there should not be finger-pointing, denial, or attempts to hide a problem. Instead, the team will want to identify any issues, adjust whatever is needed, and continue to pursue high-performance activities to realize great outcomes.

CHAPTER 9

Too Good to Be True

The Few

If you Google search "employee engagement survey results," you will see a lot of survey offers. Although most employers conduct these surveys, you'll discover that each year there are fewer than 25 percent of employers who report that they're getting good results from this process. Throughout this book I've shared my personal journey to discover my why, strengths, and values. I've also explained that clear organizational why, strength, and value awareness is vital to success. I attempted to inspire you to do the work to have this self-awareness and strategic clarity for yourself and for your organization. Finally, I shared how to bring a team together where every member of the team has figured out their personal why, strengths, and values, and I shared how when people align their why, strengths, and values with the organization's, they create a sustainable, high-performance team.

It's Simple, but It's Not Easy

There are simple steps to take to attract and inspire a high-performance team. It's not easy because you must do the work to discover your why, strengths, and values, and then work with your team to build a culture of engagement. Even though it's not easy, it's straight forward and it's worth the work.

Here are a few simple steps for maintaining a high-performance team:

1. **Choose responses that leverage strengths.**

    Once you know how to use each of your behaviors as strengths, you have the power to select the right tool for the job in stressful and challenging situations. This awareness makes it possible for you to bring a positive attitude to any situation.

2. **Lead yourself well.**

    People have agency and can engage as high-performance players once they discover their personal why, strengths, and values and lay out clear career plans. A lot of people look to their employer to design a plan and hand it to them. At this point, I'm sure you can see that a plan that someone else creates and hands to you will be based on something other than your why, strengths, and values.

3. **Be engaged.**

   If you don't invest energy in pursuing your why, using your strengths, and honoring your values, you won't be able to maintain a high performance. Bring your brain and your behavioral tools to work—be "all in."

4. **Be on time.**

   Keeping others waiting communicates that you don't value them. Punctuality is a very simple way to tell others that they matter and that you respect them.

5. **Invest the time and energy to know the why, strengths, and values of your teammates.**

   Stephen Covey (1989) said, "Seek first to understand, then to be understood." Other people are inspired when you invest time and energy in them, and people are much more interested in you after you've shown them this appreciation and respect.

6. **Seek solutions, not scapegoats.**

   One of the least productive activities for any team to engage in is laying blame or trying to cover up mistakes. Everyone makes mistakes. Laying blame doesn't solve problems. Seeking solutions invites innovation and engagement. When your team's focus is on seeking solutions, you're building a culture where people feel safe to be fully engaged. Healthy teams are comprised of people who own their mistakes and seek to help one another to solve problems.

Tend to It or It'll Become a Weed Patch

Too many organizations conduct employee engagement surveys and then fail to act on anything that they discover from the survey. Looking at the data, failure to act on engagement issues applies to around 80 percent of organizations. Whenever I'm working with leaders, I encourage them to do surveys only if they're open to acting based on what employees share. If business leaders ask questions and then do nothing, it tells employees that the boss doesn't value their input or care about them. I'm sure you can see how that message is assumed and that it makes employee engagement worse. Even if employee feedback is bad news or isn't something that the organization is prepared to change, it's important for employees to feel that they have been heard and that they get some communication related to the engagement survey.

Once you've done the work to have clarity around all the why, strengths, and values for yourself, your organization, and your team, then you'll attract and inspire your high-performance team.

Culture is like a garden that has rich soil and plenty of water. Left untended, it will grow but will become overgrown with weeds: productive but not producing what you want. If it's tended, it will produce an abundance of what you want. Your culture, like that garden, is a fertile environment. It will always produce something. If it's not tended, it may produce outcomes that aren't what you want. If it's tended, it will produce what you expect and desire at levels that may surprise you. Our approach is to bring the right tools to help you weed your culture garden and to plant the seeds that will produce an abundant harvest as a result of your gaining clear focus.

REFERENCES

Covey, Stephen R. 1989. *The 7 Habits of Highly Effective People: Powerful Lessons in Personal Change*. New York: Free Press

Harter, Jim. 2018. "Employment Engagement on the Rise in the U.S." Gallup, August 26, 2018. https://news.gallup.com/poll/241649/employee-engagement-rise.aspx.

Landemore, Hélène, and John Elster, eds. 2012. *Collective Wisdom: Principles and Mechanisms*. New York: Cambridge University Press.

Lawson, Chris, and Rob Roy. 2015. *The Navy SEAL Art of War: Leadership Lessons from the World's Most Elite Fighting Force*. New York: Crown Publishing Group.

Leimeister, Jan Marco. 2010. "Collective Intelligence." *Business & Information Systems Engineering* 2 (4): 245–248.

Morris, Massey. 1976. *What You Are Is Where You Were When*. Enterprise Media. DVD. https://www.enterprisemedia.com/product/00127/what-you-are-is-where-you-were-when---the-original.

Peters, Thomas J., and Robert H. Waterman Jr. 1982. *In Search of Excellence: Lessons from America's Best-Run Companies*. New York: Harper Business.

Sinek, Simon. 2009. *Start with Why: How Great Leaders Inspire Everyone to Take Action*. New York: Portfolio.

Strecher, Victor J. 2016. *Life on Purpose: How Living for What Matters Most Changes Everything*. New York: HarperOne.

Warren, Rick. 2002. *The Purpose Driven Life: What on Earth Am I Here For?* Grand Rapids, MI: Zondervan.

ABOUT THE AUTHOR

Brent Hultman spent years discovering how to build successful teams and to develop leaders to inspire high-performance teams. He served in Army engineer and psychological operations units, led sales and training teams, founded tech start-ups, and developed and coached leaders for small businesses, Fortune 500 companies, and local and federal government agencies. These experiences equipped Brent to diagnose problems and to apply effective, measurable solutions, solutions that he shares in this book. Brent lives in Colorado and has an active outdoor living style. He volunteers in leadership with an association of summer camps, and he has four grandchildren.

You can learn more about Brent Hultman and his services by visiting his website, brenthultmanspeaker.com.

www.ingramcontent.com/pod-product-compliance
Lightning Source LLC
LaVergne TN
LVHW041342080426
835512LV00006B/578